# KITH

# &

# KIN

# KITH & KIN

JOCELYN SAIDENBERG

THE ELEPHANTS

18 19 20 21 22 5 4 3 2 1

***



Distributed by Small Press Distribution, Inc.
Printed in Canada

***

The Elephants Ltd.
www.theelephants.net

ISBN 978-0-995-3483-9-4 print

***

*Cover image*

Johanna Drucker, *Chimp*, 2015. Watercolor and pencil.

*Interior images*

Dominique Doncre, *Petit chien jouant avec unsoulier*, 1885. Oil on canvas.

Johanna Drucker, *Ground Squirrel*, 2014. Watercolor and pencil.

Tanya Hollis, *PARCH Diptych*, 2015. Acrylic, plaster, pigment, salt and rust on wood panels.

Alice Notley, *Untitled* [*Owl for Beth*], undated. Watercolor on paper.

Azin Seraj, *Mosque-Persepolis: Concurrency Series #1*, 2014. Laser print on linen paper.

Dominique Doncre used with permission from the Musée de la Chasse et de la Nature, Paris. All other work used with permission from the artist.

Edited by Broc Rossell and Jordan Scott
Cover design by Drew Swenhaugen
Text design and typesetting by Michael Flatt

for Beth
confidante in everything

*Table of Contents*



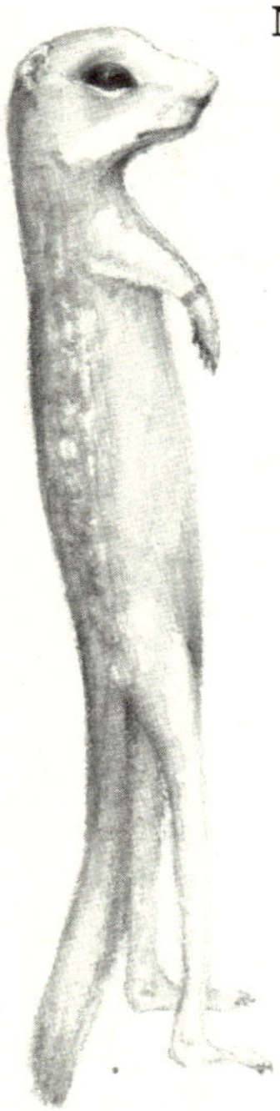

Everything was mute and calm; everything gray. The sea, though undulated into long roods of swells, seemed fixed, and was sleeked at the surface like waved lead that has cooled and set in the smelter's mould. The sky seemed a gray surtout. Flights of troubled gray fowl, kith and kin with flights of troubled gray vapors among which they were mixed, skimmed low and fitfully over the waters, as swallows over meadows before storms. Shadows present, foreshadowing deeper shadows to come.

—HERMAN MELVILLE

(By music we mean sound; but what's time? Certainly not that something begins and ends.)

—JOHN CAGE

I was a hawk before this –
I was collecting incredible views
The song of our brief encounter

—BETH MURRAY

## SEPTEMBER

it's the mist
it's an oak titmouse in the feeder
it's not a privation a list
of what not to do but the no
vote's loss is depressing
what would have united
by rending that delight
of negation to hold where
one wants to attract the bait
of cunning napping with Beth
who's all bone & lumps the days
are shortening her "night's
night" come memory
an artless shape better
dwell in disorder with dust

## SEPTEMBER

Azin erased the bills cleansed
of numerals rubbed off remains
in valueless landscapes composing signs
to shed in lieu of exchanging
in currencies in space less figure
to cipher her image a longwise
rectangle whose proportions ought money

mistake air for or & breath for alternative
signed yours in the sink stinks of value
unearthed the old notebooks filled
with leaving & pattern who've grown
mold under ought & foxing

> when the sun storms so hide
> inside clench land & sky
> gathered & immobile
> what I had read for
> immoral I ought to or
> I ought to ago what
> owes to my owing
>
> torn in the flesh or thorn in the fish
> & Daniel thinks my plan subverts
> the problem but so does his

## SEPTEMBER

after us invariably
moon mass
that song of infinite
family its heart mongering
for winter for hamstrung emotional

not where I thought it would be
that super moon's
still hid
then Gus vomits at dawn
just before light a pile of rocks &
tawny pine needles
one mass hits
another bigger mass & that mass spits
out audibly some mass from its inside
rotating like a tennis ball but
larger makes a moon to be
resultant voices redouble
because it is more because it is
weighty who both resounds
& makes more mass happen

to fill the whole
land with wailing first
rending & low for there's
much more in store for Reeva
apparently ran legally into four bullets

who departed her mortally

        a naked lament first of all
that excludes even mourners

        when a face on a cover
I mistake for tears & hers repeatedly
what moot person whose twin of another

## SEPTEMBER

built into a hillside by months
& mold holding earth
                    there's a fox
who rooms there
weighing the costs of
living in degrees of heat
that invade from
inside to possess a false
sky that disarms it with witchcraft
in degrees popping up in refusals
in movement figured
in the time it takes to starve

                                                            it rained
last night cleaning away old
habits of summer old friends whose
living confines a difference
too great for a chapter
there's no point in starting
something with no
promise & that's not rhetorical
it's literal
                                                                            & it's
too stupid to list those with whom
& a stupid list of losses those who abandoned
the dead & those whose suffering
held them possessed like those owls do

Dee Dee's cat Dodie is dying all fur
& bone like Beth she can't retract her claws
any longer so Mari helps her off my shoulder

it's new year's once more so
conjure anew why any name
is ours to be written

## OCTOBER

equivalence isn't the same as existence
or the same as living or you can go now
flushed out from the shrubbery
to a surface whose angle is
moving toward you & yours
& your dying
                                but the moths *are* the moths
eating wool blankets & flying round
the desk light too tenderly to escort
a walrus herd in flight toward that lapse
like some dolphins do

          *nil igitur mors est ad nos*

to walk facing into a spider's
web along the garden path & left there
this spider astride the shipwreck
of what I can't avoid
          that being oneself can't be
being self possession of one who can't
seed a self whose being who
oneself
          now can't mean one

## OCTOBER

she's begun to hallucinate
she's talking with the dead & her brother
who's dead & she's begun
          there's a deep vibrating
          noise oscillating
banging through miles of air from far off
all I can't tell her any longer separated
by more than intervals I want what
she wants & she wants it tomorrow
she's already near & there

it's unremarkable to remark on
how strange the weather is
a constant state of withiness
is like saying to remark that want
is need is as remarkable as the weather
she gets what she wants
under a full moon she makes
her heart stop
no longer that body
or pain that thrives
on living

          a prediction without signs
          & with owl eyes
she fixes her gaze on something

off & that eventual breath
nothing else would work
no invention
                                        for the lion's
share is everything

## OCTOBER

fewer birds are bolder coming closer
as curiosity's companion for light
interloped & poaching
no longer that self

            I did repair the hole in the rug
with the tools she'd given me
I did repair the breach with Bob
when horrible things happen
the smallest lapse an insult felt

but when intensity
lessens which is worse
to pause to remember to remember

            reading disorder for order
humiliation for friendship for what
guarantor that authors for Martial
making a book makes the book a debt
for its maker & that's literal when
what grows augmented
towards
those makers of matter
then I look with solicitude
& console the impossible

## OCTOBER

I buy flowers two bunches
Norma says she eats chocolate
for those ones who can't any
longer I translate *pastor*
*cum traheret* for the shame
of having horrible things happen
forsaking this vividness it costs
too much for tenderly living

no stars no moon it's
been two weeks & she's
still traveling she feels
more away more distant
redundant & it's her
syntax of pattern
& prayer that's
hocus pocus
*hoc est corpus*
*meum pro vobis*

but not now unraveling
for fox for fox for

              to shepherd her
across the waves in her
idea boat in a song
as her atmosphere of promise

an apostrophe to future
I stumble into this where
atoms split I rescue
objects it's my duty I
leave things as they are as
if to be summoned I remind
myself that she can't

to conclude Alice performs
her ritual of outrage a ceremony
for those who no longer yet
who had hungered
she didn't remember
the drawing she'd drawn
of an owl in flight
but only the owl feather
that Beth sent
that her drawing
in reply was sent for

## OCTOBER

it'd be a distraction to build one
          for her
I'm pretty certain Beth has what she needs
          & lacks for nothing no wanting
          no obstacles
how long does she travel? I could
          call someone to find out
          the number but won't
I don't know how to take stock
          a privilege not to know or faith
          there will be enough & even almost
          enough
if there's stock it's messy
          too many going & uncertain
          arrivals animals changing places changing
          spellings even the sky's disarranging
          heavy on top
for less weighing correspondence
          is composed in an order
          already less knowing
there's an error in a change of address
          that the name of the book is also
          to address someone absent
          that is the title is the absent
          name I can't remember
she'd wanted to know how to do it
          to be in concert in a poem

in flight she'd wanted
to talk about poetry
& she'd wanted to listen
to owls talk about poetry
to be solicitous to the unlikely
to make for more listening for
beings absent in concert
I'm pretty certain she'd want to

## NOVEMBER

[organs] I've done something to my left hip the rubber band that attaches my leg to my trunk is twisted or just worn thin. I sent a message to her wrote a letter in light sealed it with stars for some shells. I found a tree whose trunk was capacious & I hung her letter on the trunk on whose other side was another message to another Beth also recently dead. I saw the moon several times it's waxing again its heaviness sleeps on my chest pulling inward like that was love.

*

[labors] Judith helps me make a list of inventory the boxes of books & number of books & kinds of totals & there are some that have none add one that is gone completely fucked gladly. I give her the fragrance she'd wanted but couldn't discover & later my relief in finding the Brabants who are mentioned infrequently are the same Brabants I knew so well from the opera.

*

[weather] this angle of sun makes no effort to warm what lazy star in the car I told Judith & Norma about Sam telling me about Bernadette who lived next door in New York & Norma told us she's been married four times with two wedding dresses. Clark Coolidge told us it took him many years to see foreigner in for Eigner. Why don't they have water for the readers at such a moneyed venue & I want to vomit when men are mentioned by last names but women by first, i.e. Creeley & Bernadette. I travel back with Evan his body & gestures are memory in his affective collection but he'd never say it like that. I am immobile with a sadness that makes me.

*

[mistranslations] of all the strawmen I want to rescue it's the one who's most textured, who flattens the least that leads to what's not already & by vias unknown to the strawmen of history to the strawmen of everyday that I want to retake. But I misrecognize the tense emphatically. It's an imperfect not perfect & I'd have to return all my library books & write awkward notes. Incompatible grief. Its conflict with living.

*

[inventories] the road out was a river dried not flowing with standing water in puddles & polished rocks not hard to navigate by foot where there were infrequent others like marchers following it downstream to a source of darkness an endwise entrance below. I held a dog who was dying gathered to my body I repeated *it's okay you can go now* at the end of the river road in the shadows of limit a whole dog being taken catching as much fur & mass in my arms she left while some returned upstream surprising I stayed at the mouth to an otherwise I knew by her fur it was Beth before she was sick letting me help her die once more no holding back on a path beyond to an entrance where she went this mouth to an elsewhere.

*

[birdbrain] there's a sequence called time: she's sick, she dies, she's still dead, no matter the voice, passive or active, but the other won't have it that way not in that order or tense. It figures apprehension & owing. No promise or debt to pursue. Is it like grains of sand? like stars? what's myriad? Not quite, without senses. Then while reading the letter by Bruce I find a compositional circle ringing & containing that draws us together.

*

## NOVEMBER

less the more not exactly
a pair not oblivious either but
not familiar the less I do
the more she is or the more I
sleep the less she is not or the less
light less love to trust to live
if not to person a dream
we're winking so Beth kings it
because she's making
a racket repairing a bucket
will they let us keep what makes
it most alien is to unkind it
being with what before what is
found as a dirge for before what
we court to keep measuring
distances & inward longing
for extremes to count
that no one go hungry
all hallucinate nightly
it's difficult being

against being
the more now
the less to undo it

## NOVEMBER

The non-culinary thyme plant I bought the day she died
    has died too.
I need help with everything.
I can hear the clock grinding time but that's literal
    so I unplug it.
I'm lagging behind trying to redo what couldn't
    be done—I till but don't sow.
To read one thing as another & the other as always
    the other but what if it is itself local & not
    withdrawing then to lose won't reply but is
    just losing.
It rained. It's raining now.
To be on the floor & then on your knees you ache
    for your songs repeat you roundly
    you offer to fall lest you avoid
    the inward losses from sounding

## NOVEMBER

it's singular unless fewer
it's plurals except less
not for what self
if there's only
until empty
only more flesh
for the telling
that's
what makes
the rock plural to
itself for
                    you can't
have everything says
the owl whose barred
chest sings in late fall

to lose the insult
of being more
to lose the bloom
of a place a fox
who moves

slowly stunned
by the rain to
build a tomb
for the holidays
is the life of
slumber

animals & fur
breathing bodies
coiled inwards
the life of tilling
neither planting
nor sowing
habits repeating
wasting for turning
tonight still raining
that sleep at rest
these bodies who
sound yet love in
extremity

## DECEMBER

now the other plant that I bought
for her on that day is under attack
            these impossible
leaves laced into themselves
with furried stalks being eaten
by someone I've tried pepper & soap
but each morning it's still more
diminished I've learned all

her chickens
are dead too
taken & eaten
one by one by foxes
for everyone's hungry

                        in stone
those whose mistakes hunger finds
no relief for to end yet again
why more for them than for others
the full moon again & what punctures
a limit each day more diminished
regardless the pepper regardless the soap
fallen for falling instead repeatedly
                        the rain
is prodigious not the drudge of narration
or confession of image neither living

nor keeping I've lost
the pretext or what's obvious by
absence even in this instance
the foxes are literal
like shades like those who

## DECEMBER

our ever friend, Green, you
who arrange the alphabet by shapes
who gag on machines who are
swamp & vomit who choke
on smiles who float & flood
who enumerate synonyms in flight
in lists declining the trees in likeness
fields of seedling leaving for once
there were no less no more nothings
in hurricanes your light repeating
                                        & by you, Green, accrue
patterns departed with voicings
without notice a mouth now listening
sideways listing ever to love
                                                    may we figure in fleeing
                                                    forms of sorrows
owing for you, Green, we will do it
without stop without end to make
if not likely an address to place it

## DECEMBER

This drama of being a being threatened by being always in
peril of not being not given no longer decided & in
non-guarantee of horizon of each also still a problem.

I have problems.
I'm thinking in circles.
The fruit rots on the ground in the rain better to be a being
returned to ashes is asking.
Mold going from golden to blue deflating the flesh of
horizon when it was still a possible problem to have.

I gave more than I had because the rain returns to the
ground. It's grammatical.
They let you in & they let you there.

For utterance changes the utterer.
I feel certain of that for the time being.
In the face of another not the other way round.

## DECEMBER

on what is not
is not nothing
not there is no
thing yet nothing
is like no other
nothing upon rising
to feel & to mark
an impression in
inches of light
are slower
like odd numbers
who extra
who wait
for blood oranges
to decouple weather
& season
not grammar who owes
obscurity in shading
*adieu* to the glamour
of clouds & rings within
rings within clearings

*Cent Sept* for sunset to resolve
the holes ties up & lets go
the phrase once gone leaves
the broken broken under charm
the other of confusing
the gas for the break

next season to come
will come after this one
under the tree trunk
this bark who departed

## JANUARY

je suis for sleeping
missing then turning
a goat with her bar-
coded fleece all wooly
whose initials je
suis lost then
prickles along
not reliably
ergo the drought

je suis she it
seems enormous
trails thru sky to your
undisclosed bird
feeder je suis crumbs

no longer does strife
make eloquent je
but je suis
swallows under
trickling of suis
after binding for
espionage je coding

Beth's aunt prays for us:

*be barren!*

*o, you circular lovers*
nous somme suis

shift perspectives je je who
were unknowing somme

## JANUARY

unwashed upsets
my listening within
witness delirious brackets
I meant listing a sudden
all the last leaves
are fallen with old
blotches & reflex
not seeming
felt more frequent
on all sides tight
with change
there the mountain
lions line the cold
interfering with pronouns
I am a person with
problems
                    century
for cemetery to bury
no relation
                    looking it
up for my substance
space reverses

: do you wear a belt?
: yes, to hold up my pants.
: glad to hear it, friend.

stop digging
the germs are all home

put your house key
in your change purse
when you're far from
the owls whenever
wherever stay close

for they sleep sleepers
& dream dreamers utterly
for what they could say if
there were no sleeper
no dreamer none under

to tame with feelings
thought's thoughts

## JANUARY

missing tether
lost for recapture
receptive for weather
for two cats overheated
that's block for deficit for
raining for cleaving
& I still need help with
everything
            I can't
defend myself from myself
for my own friends
            our tides overwriting
the flooding inflowed & dizzy
for being more for the less
for misnaming stupid
in the first place
to trust so much in weather

that copter overhead
& in my head tells me to
write to her brother
or maybe her aunt to ask
how to live when to plant
with advice & instruction

## FEBRUARY

        why that hidden sharp stick
or refuge

again cyphering
a mollusk house against
an inked sky in
frequencies

a listening life in my head & among
sounds organizing uneven skin
        infrequently
        echo of an echo   a reminder
hidden
remains hidden

her words over & move away
inks off sepia cuttlefish housing
nocturnal remedies from Beth
both cloistered & endearing
owl & octopus familiars
luminous unbounded anti
gravitational dark & reclusive

my old boss avoids me at the market
I was the problem in his head smirking

who cooks for you?
who cooks for you?
accumulator

mischief for circular
for day say season
who cooks for you?

## FEBRUARY

address the charges
for snout in mouth
for riding high there
nothing supplies
practice passing along
in counting & now
the forth full moon
gray owl gone

love — won't you catch
cold in that dress

likely returns
when it rains
when it's just dark
*repetitio mater memoriae*

as preface to dolphins
at anchor as practice
why delete what grows
to surpass it by ships
among pebbles & waves
born but to perish
what it knows
to return *festina lente*
another candle for Rex
when it's raining

## FEBRUARY

resonant in his own voice Rex cries
"Silky!" holding up his dear captive point
by point sembling dog for dog & in likeness
fox & owl & kith & kin as whirlwinds referring
in rumors removed from names outside
turned in first letters go under for forgotten
then gaps then falls in assembly

## FEBRUARY

assaults on continuous
understorms offered often
that was suitors for sutures
that's a stone weeping
for inwardness meant that's
ever but couldn't less
than last time lamenting

these singers repeating *DER TOD*
*DER TOD TOD TOD*
for I hear you through
my sound tunnel
crying at unwanted no no no
no not you inaudible

the owl
stay close to the owl
stay close

## MARCH

to attend to what's missing
what hasn't happened
who's not here &
there marks a faint voicing
between dust & what
rustles after crumple to
infold the traces having
already what once ago then

it's okay just to

maybe close for nearness
what's rustling homes branches
missing the tracks then stops
what's remaining left
then stops without
what's willed indwelt
when nesting under
all sound of matter
then rests then stops

## MARCH

to but forget & better yet to oblivion
in rhythms that storm the living & after which none

no to doubtless
no to skills & pills
no to talking with those who don't
no to asking those who don't
no to those who don't

giving more bird song now than
last time getting more to come
with those who don't & after which none

spit on often & loudly
gist for bit & these problems
where there are not none
probably today not possible

what I can't remember & haven't
what I am not doing & chose not to & don't

## MARCH

after invariably my finger
digs in artifice & I had a plan

to land the land
sky the sky & give
to the sea for donations

myself living to a time
for to hear it from
rivers diversify & fly
the north storm
where be ineloquence

when wolf
with sheep
where owl
among fox
whereas being
stones for bones
who with regards
yet among us

## APRIL

sequestered in proximate
shadows not touching
whose ink ends in accounts
who copy catastrophes
whose unlikely
eclipsing a day off
deferred in refusal
                    just stop face
flushing in public
where mistaking touch
for being yet seeming
not memorized
but forgetting ergo
not finding for refinding
what can't gap
won't otherwise not
having & still wanting
passes on something
obscene like early
retirement for every silent
tout yclept airdancers in flight
flapping for capital vested
lower-case frantic in attention
unlikely but bumps
into bumps non-stop
seasonal ailment
forecasting the same dying

suppose it fudges it
seems more or less similar
fallen under why not
wait until after pat
pat pat repeated
o, drought be anonymous
another not not nor likely

## APRIL

Hunger has moss
inside lining her throat
feeding there & she shows
up with black eyes
for a bland guide
her face near transparent
over more in wanting but
less overcast for I like
to think you as maybe but
underfigured again & now

still shifting round
in time lately planted
iterative fumbling of tenses
budding & leafing to ask
why there's a predicate
but can't predict it
neither enough nor often

as if a refrain a return
of that phrase to mark out
our surrounding for shelter
when storms gust impressive
to hold it Beth used to suggest
like a small animal in your arms
against your chest she'd very often
suggest as if it already had to

## MAY

already statistical
lists as laments stupidly
in ledgers naked containers
in horizon to margins whenever
rests up returns elsewhere

reading what follows
in lieu of those who
remember to remember
on palindrome days
ask for more help

                                        once I
fasted on watermelon
near Toronto with Misha
to attend birdsong hymns
in an ill-illuminated
clearing where I found
comprehension in words
without recollection

## MAY

My nerves hurt. That's literal.
Judith tells me to think positive. She says "It really helps."
I hear in my head a neutered child who's flushing & urgent
all over & passing for someone.
I dislike the heat & I pee on it.
Apples index & they heard me trash it.
Stop showing off!
You just passed.

## MAY

this uphill remainder
neither aims nor amounts

Beth for Gus
who kills a bird
finch not sparrow
sonic not shape

who sends
a wrong message
instinct not object

I set the bird body
dead among fennel
food for another
in a not empty lot
for everyone is
hungry still

on the last day of the year
under the heading of dead
in spirals not to be shared
Bhanu dreamed of Beth
in a nest not with strangers
she now tells me assembled

for in the event that something
befalls me while 'borrowing'
roses from somebody's garden
for those dearly let me
scatter there seedlings
to dwell in dust

## JUNE

abstraction renounces dirt
ergo disembodies her textures
of glamour—magic & rhetoric
so literally I hate it

let's decivilize with unreason for the sake of
Moppsy the cat who died before catsitting
in person only possible in kind

when with fragmented family
other losses are mortal so
adding some two times
this iteration of what
if what's chosen

if headaches twin
my refuge in scandal

my note to my neighbors:

Your straight asses fucking makes me wanna puke!!!!!!
You don't own the air, Bitches!!!!!!
Take it inside!!!!!
—A neighbor

(I nailed it to this door in my head)

## JUNE

*Exeo* but how? Ask her main verb?
Where is her main verb? When will I see her main verb at last?
What will her main verb hear today? Tomorrow?
Will her main verb walk in the streets in shadows? Will rain be her main verb?

I untie the bone from my neck to breathe better & I win at poker. All in.
For all are accountable. For bodies for yours. No exceptions none. Repeat.

There are more than two types of people but there are those people who divide people into types.
Usually two types.
As if only one leads & one follows.
As if only one is & one isn't.
But bodies already protest.
A walking refusal instead side by side with the dead.

## JUNE

mistakes proceed then follow
on the map itself & elsewhere
being thought right & wrong
but finally inaccessible in wanting
gray owl for holding

            her last handful
given to the river
filling green circles
below sways under
            then caught by the wind
her ashes of cloud meeting my hands
gesturing greeting & farewell
then from afar to those who

except
for the smell
not hers but ash
just ash

when night finds me
organizing sounds like figures
differently less densely like pronouns
like fingers
like many fingers on many hands
to account for the ones already who

## JULY

The mob *is* right

            no question in
this instance because need
to know is intel whereas
nice to know is gossip
what all worldly rumor
makes possible when
earth is a table luring
in postures not neutral
where there's no nomination
for the owls already know
this is this

who unbind the books in a space-
time migration from paper
to moment in flight & it's off
again in ink & in rustlings with
what longing recounting swallows

for if numbers aren't language
but magic if nothing
how then to turn to
what moves beyond figures

## AUGUST

We were by the stream discussing subjection when the pigs
showed up.
That's literal.
That's what the owl knows too.

Once crowded like raisins but how now the storm ends for
herself.
Nothing else would do.
No more nobody or anybody, but bodies not the body a
body.
No more no one no thing any thing, for my plots are friends
with myriad bodies instead.
For instance a radius redoubled, but that's not a figure.

See instead we are themselves waves, no longer figured,
carried or held under but assemblies in unending seas
where shepherded by dolphins we are of them that are we &
that is what the owl knows.

## AUGUST

elaboration as in
let's be limp
or let's only sow
yet in shadows

attend to what's porous
in duration who endure

in gashes then
after a respite
eat sounds
over naming
abide in alliance

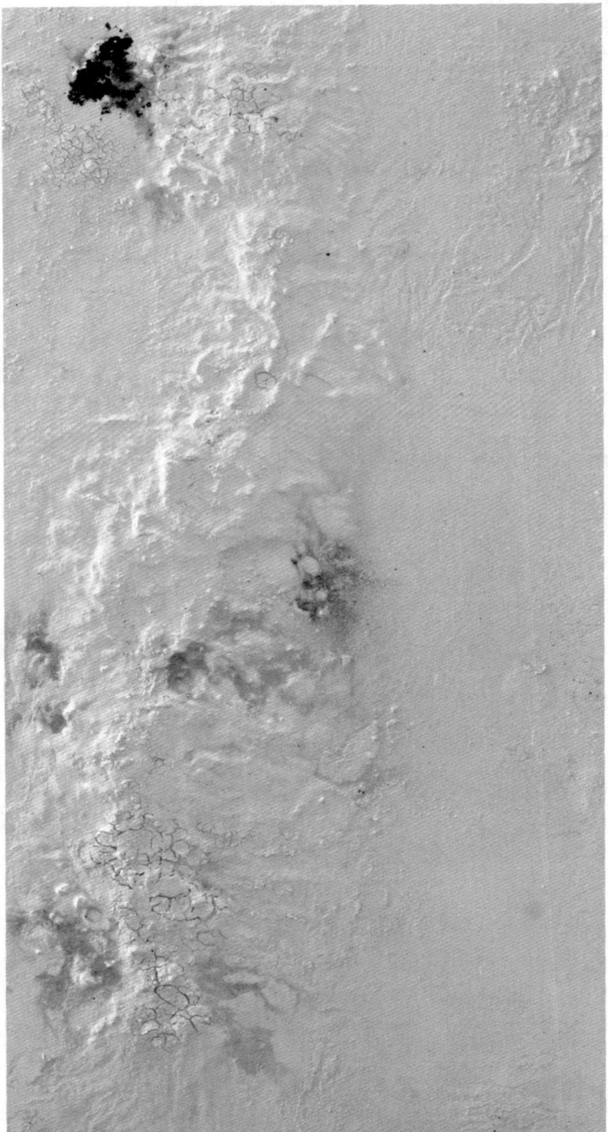

## AUGUST

There's smoke in the sky from fires burning all over the state.
Now smoke mixes with cloud.
Now wind colludes with matter.
I lost one of the feet of what I had made to be practical.
For what purpose would it have a purpose now?
Now would it be improvident to plan for the future without
regard for weather, fires, clouds or matter? There is no reply.
Repair & restuff the old friendships for furniture I suggest as
if that had never occurred to Bruce, which as it turned out it
hadn't. For he cares little for the stuff of life as Bob calls it. I
know too much about that like Bob who does too.
This will be the time to repeat to myself repair & restuff.
Yedda says she could.
So with my lip I cover the missing tooth as if hiding from notice.
Can abstract be lost? I could write a letter, maybe.
It would have two names, mine & yours, no more no less
between, if there's nothing to say or too much. Is that abstract?
A trickle isn't soothing, isn't something.
Bruce who's written a love letter to Carter with brain cancer,
says better than screaming.
Like neither nor ever there's nothing to it to like.

## AUGUST

I remind myself what's lost
will not return or while
the odds aren't good it's
not impossible like
either summer smoker
or smoked one summer
or some new national holidays
are unlikely like
Day of Alliance
Day of Protest
Day of Dying
Day of Madness & Unreason
Palindrome Day
Ritual Day
Day-off Day

disorder for perception
when I reward myself
with rewards then it's
not theoretical but
to remove from the trail
what obstacles which if not
grammatical solely
can't feel more
abstractly its having been
lived & now not & now yet

with restraint
my ears find refrain
returned under

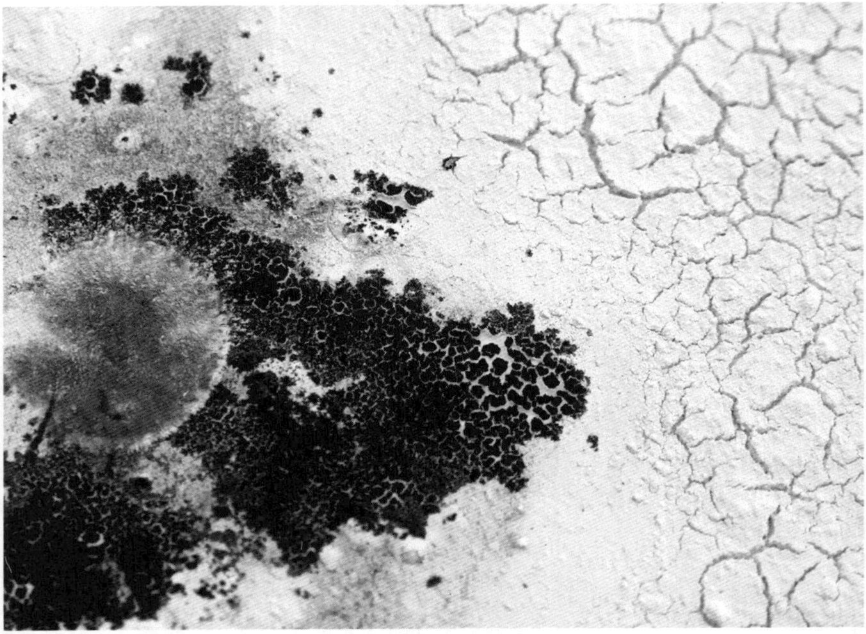

*some notes*

*Kith & Kin* is born of a desire to write about what I tend to deny or avoid: my body, my organizational obsessions, the banality of my everyday, my mistakes and messes, that is, my desire to invite the exclusions in and to entertain the excess. By attending to what my attention resists, my inattention, I had the hunch that in approaching my withdrawal, shame, and omissions, I might find myself in proximity to others, ones who mumble, who yell in rage, who are recently or long dead, who dream me at night, those who are lost to me, yet whose beings compose my beings. As Judith Butler writes: "I find that my very formation implicates the other in me, that my own foreignness to myself is, paradoxically, the source of my ethical connection with others." We are traversed by others, by their traces and impressions. Who we are is never fully knowable, for we constitute an assembly of others and selves. In this sense, the writing summons and is summoned by others collectively, enigmatically as our elaboration of losses and assemblies.

*acknowledgements*

My thanks to Allison Cardon for publishing a portion of an earlier version of this text in *P-QUEUE* 14 and for suggesting the title. Thanks to Broc Rossell and Jordan Scott for their support, their pencil-sharp editorial suggestions and enthusiasm.

Conversations with friends and their work inform everything I write. My deepest thanks to these steadfast interlocutors—Robert Glück, Stephanie Young, Eric Sneathen, Yedda Morrison, Norma Cole, Rob Halpern, Daniel Benjamin, Lyn Hejinian, Camille Roy, Pam Martin, Bruce Boone, Anne Walsh, Syd Staiti, Samantha Giles, Mia Maturin, Michelle Koerner, Judith Goldman, Eliot D'Silva and Rebeca Bolinger.

I am grateful to Tanya Hollis and Azin Seraj for their art works, to Alice Notley for the owl drawing that she made for Beth and that Beth left to me, and to Johanna Drucker for the cover art and ground squirrel inside.